School Holidays

by Marta Fuentes
illustrated by Sandy Kossin

Harcourt

Orlando   Boston   Dallas   Chicago   San Diego

Visit *The Learning Site!*
www.harcourtschool.com

Everywhere students go to school.
Everywhere students learn to read.
Everywhere students learn numbers.
Everywhere students learn to write.
Everywhere students take time out to play.
Everywhere students take time off from
school to celebrate holidays!

The school year has started. Students have new classrooms. Students have new teachers and new classmates. They have new books to read.

They use new pens and pencils to write. Students write words and numbers.

It is fun to learn and to play each day.

In many places in the world, children get breaks from school to celebrate holidays.

This class is learning about an American holiday in October.

The holiday is Columbus Day. In 1492, Christopher Columbus sailed from Spain. He sailed west to find India.

Columbus had no maps. He was very brave.

Christopher Columbus used three ships: the Niña, the Pinta, and the Santa María.

Columbus was looking for India, but he found America instead. He went to Cuba, Haiti, Puerto Rico, and parts of South America. He and his men made some maps.

On Columbus Day, we think about how Columbus's voyages changed the Americas. People have parades. Some schools are closed on this holiday, but students still learn about Columbus and his travels.

This class is learning about another American holiday. The holiday is Thanksgiving. It takes place in November. On this happy holiday, people think about the Pilgrims. Long ago, the Pilgrims moved to a new land—America. Everything was new. Native Americans helped the Pilgrims.

The new land did not have towns. It did not have roads or stores. People grew their food. They made their houses.

On the first Thanksgiving, the Native Americans and Pilgrims ate a special meal together. They gave thanks for their food.

On Thanksgiving, people take time off from work and school to spend time with their families and friends. This is a time for people to give thanks for food and all good things.

This class is learning about an African-American holiday. This holiday is called Kwanzaa.

It is a very happy holiday in December. Kwanzaa takes place for seven days and nights.

On Kwanzaa, people give thanks. They give thanks for good food. They give thanks for good health. They give thanks for their families.

During Kwanzaa, people light seven candles.
People light one candle each night. People sing
songs and dance. People eat a big dinner with
their families. At Kwanzaa, everyone wishes for
a happy new year!

Many businesses and schools are closed for
winter holidays. During this time people can
celebrate Kwanzaa.

This class is getting ready for Tet. Tet is a new year holiday. People who come from Vietnam celebrate this holiday.

Tet always takes place in January or February. During this holiday, people celebrate their birthdays and give thanks for their families and their health. People give gifts in red paper. Children are happy to get gifts in red paper.

During Tet, people put up a Cay Neu, or New Year's tree. This tree is a bamboo pole with all the leaves removed except for a few at the top. The tree is decorated with red paper.

People take the time during Tet to remember their relatives and to be kind to each other.

This class is learning about a Mexican holiday. People who come from Mexico celebrate this holiday. The holiday is Cinco de Mayo.

Cinco de Mayo means "May 5" in Spanish. This holiday is about freedom.

Some schools and businesses are closed for Cinco de Mayo. During this holiday, people sing songs and students put on plays.

Cinco de Mayo is a happy holiday. Everyone eats good food. Everyone dances. Everyone has fun!

This class is learning about another American holiday, Memorial Day. This holiday comes at the end of May.

On Memorial Day people remember the brave men and women who fought and died for their country.

People take a break from work and school to show respect for soldiers who died while serving America.

On Memorial Day people have parades.
Many people in the military march in these
parades. The people who watch the parades feel
very patriotic, or proud of their country. People
fly the American flag on this holiday.

It is important to remember the reason for a holiday. A holiday is a time to come together with family and friends. A holiday is a time to remember where you come from. A holiday is a time to remember an important person or event. Holidays are special, no matter which ones you celebrate.